Bitty Bear

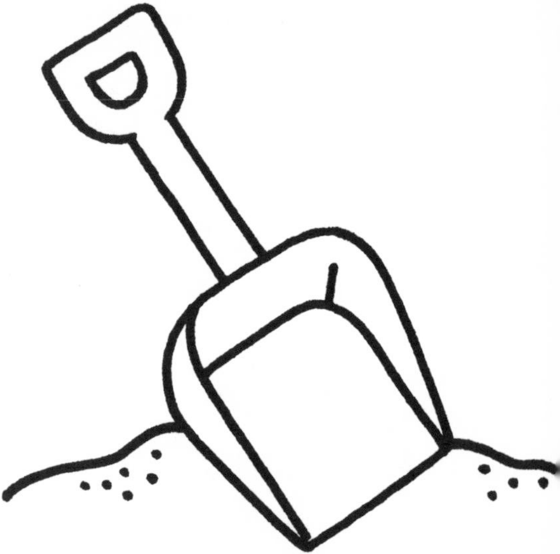

shovel

butterfly

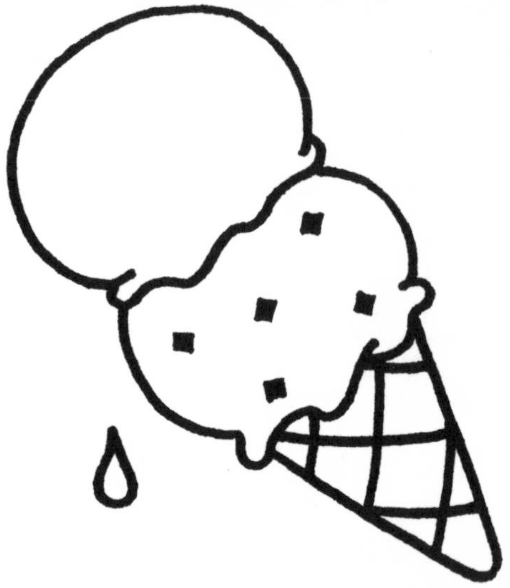

ice cream cone

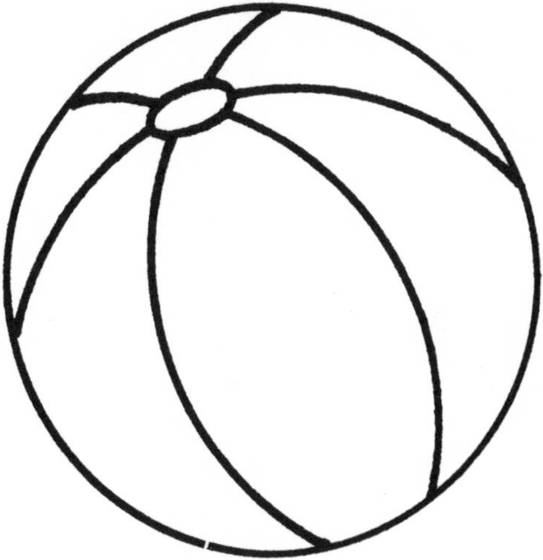

beach ball

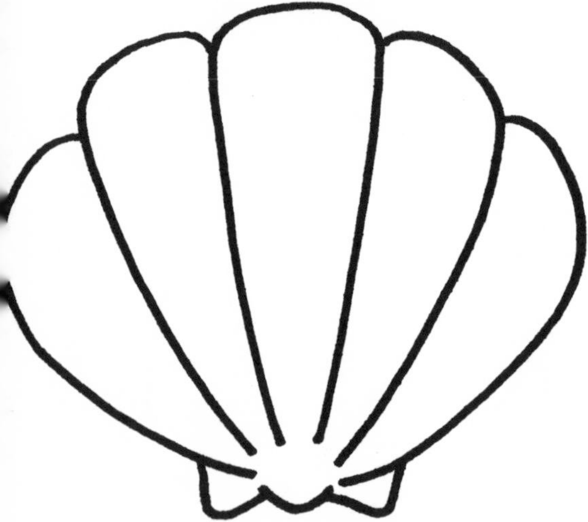

shell

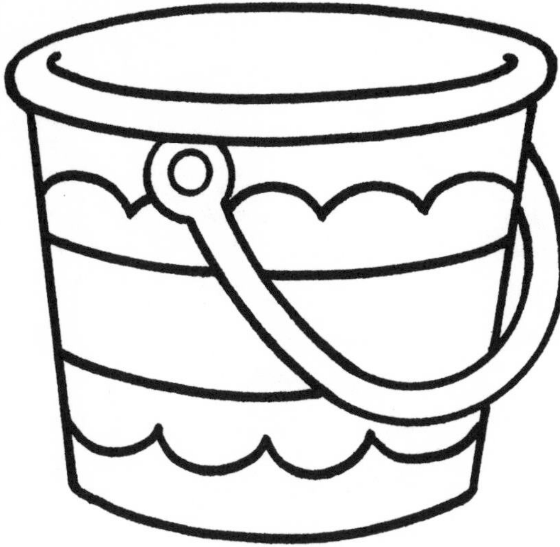

pail

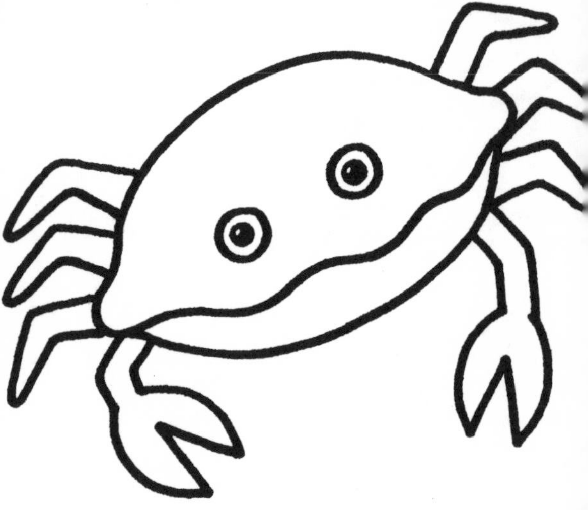

crab

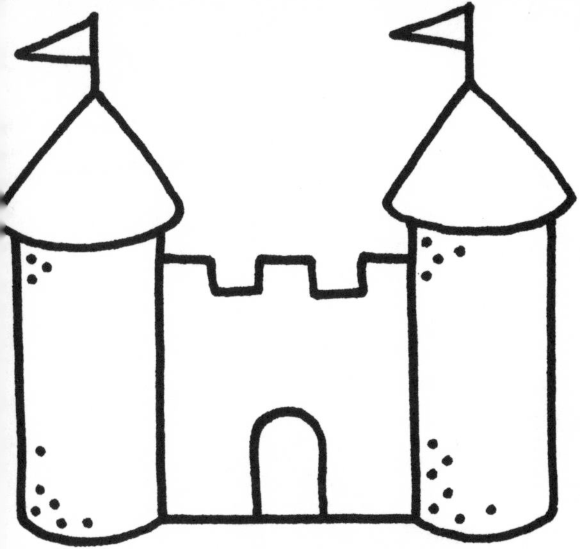

sand castle

starfish

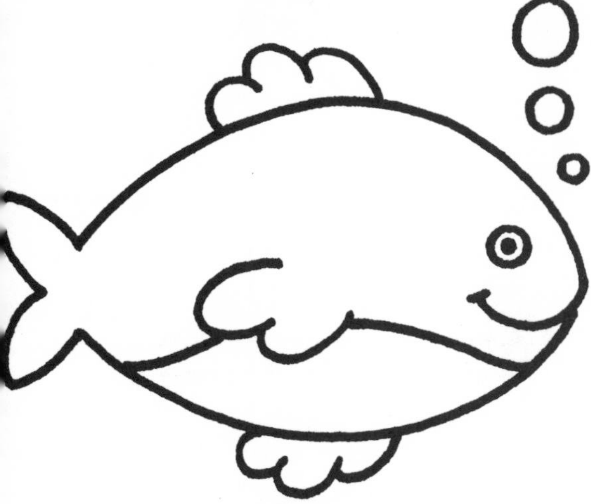

fish

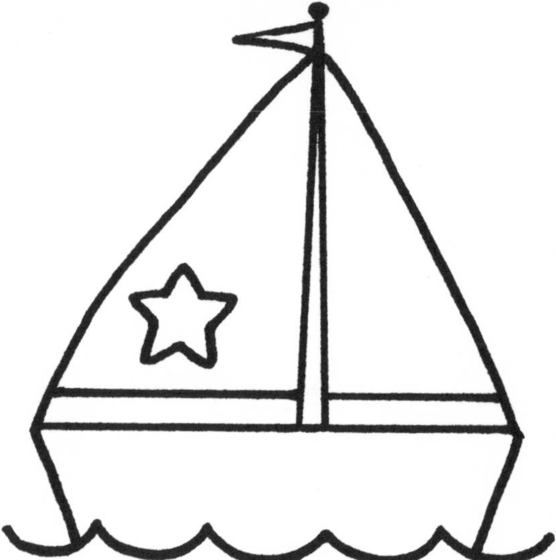

sailboat